P9-APR-170

HUE™

BOOK OF

ANIMATION

How to make movie magic
John Cassidy & Nicholas Berger

TABLE OF CONTENTS

Model Car Smashups
(page 16)

The Nightmare Before
Breakfast (page 20)

No-Handed Eating
(page 22)

Duck, Duck, Poop
(page 30)

Lawn Skating
(page 34)

Magic Shoes
(page 38)

How To Make Nigel Take A
Fall (page 46)

Space Hero
(page 48)

Unmelting Ice Cream
(page 50)

The Book

The book is half of the story. It's the instructions and backstage tour. It contains all of the secrets that you'll need to make the animated videos described in the chapters below.

The Videos

The other half of the story is the collection of videos. Each of them is available to watch on the CD included in HUE Animation Studio. You can also watch them online at **www.hueanimation.com/creations**

Runaway Clay
(page 24)

Clay Hero
(page 26)

Clayvolution
(page 28)

How to Fly
(page 40)

Paper Doll Disco
(page 42)

Famous Fruit Speeches
(page 44)

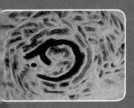

Sand Snake
(page 52)

Magical Moving Family
Photos (page 54)

Rotoscoping
(page 58)

The Most Popular Magic Trick of All Time

I'm alive!

In the real world, things are sort of boring: Chairs don't walk, brooms don't fly, mice don't talk, and little clay characters don't have fun adventures.

But in the world of animation, things are very different.

Animation is an optical trick that relies on the fact that our eye/brain connection can only do so much. If you were watching an ordinary slide show, and then dialed up the speed until the pictures were running fast enough, they would start to blur together. Call it the brain's speed limit. Somewhere around 10 fps (frames per second) the gaps between the pictures disappear and the picture starts to "move" (making "movies").

About 150 years ago, a couple of people figured out the trick of animation could be used to create some moving picture toys, unpronounceably called "thaumatropes," "zoetropes," and "phenakistoscopes." Check out our print-out activity sheets for a ratty version of a phenakistoscope that you can cut out and use!

Thaumatrope, the beginnings of animation

Phenakistoscope

How to make lumps of clay sing and dance.

How to make paper dolls fly through outer space.

CLAYMATION

CUT-OUT ANIMATION

How to make eggs scurry around the house.

How to make a photograph go for a walk.

OBJECT ANIMATION

Isn't Animation Just a Fancy Word for Cart👀ning?

Cartooning (where a series of drawings is made to come alive) is just one flavor of animation. Thanks to Mickey Mouse and Bart Simpson, people tend to think it's the only one. But "traditional cell animation" (as it's technically called) is just the most common style; there are many more. For example, in this book, we're going to be doing...

PHOTO ANIMATION

How to make people move in magical ways.

How to make animation speed up snails.

TIME LAPSE

PIXILATION

How to turn video into animation.

ROTOSCOPING

DIFFICULTY LEVEL
1

DIFFICULTY LEVEL
2

DIFFICULTY LEVEL
3

Easy　　Medium　　Tricky

The Three Steps of Animation

1. Take a picture of something.
2. Change it.
3. Shoot it again.

Regardless of the technique used, or the thing drawn or photographed, animation can always be boiled down to three steps:

1. Take a still picture of something (a drawing, a banana, a guy on the lawn...).
2. Change it a little bit.
3. Shoot it again.

Repeat.

When you run all the little still pictures together in front of your eyes very quickly, the magic appears: The banana sings, the guy flies, the drawing runs around.

How to perform these miracles is what the rest of this book is about.

What Do I Need to Start?

A USB camera is an important tool for stop motion animation. It lets you view your stage and characters live while you take pictures. This means that you can correct mistakes and delete frames as you go along. If you prefer, you can take pictures with any digital camera or camcorder and import them into the animation software later. Be careful though - doing this means that you can't easily fix a problem or mistake.

Connecting the HUE camera

The HUE camera can be connected to the computer's USB port without needing a driver. As soon as the camera has been connected and recognized, it's ready for use and you can launch the animation software. You can use it with its base and cable, or plug the camera's flexible neck straight into a laptop's USB port. For extra help setting up your HUE camera, visit **www.huehd.com**

Setting up your stage

Set up your backdrop and place your characters in front of the camera. If you're using a paper backdrop, make sure that it's secured to the table with tape or putty, then position your camera in front of the stage and turn the focusing ring until the picture is sharp.

Making up a story

You can use a storyboard template to plan your movie by drawing simple pictures describing what happens and what your characters say. You can print a blank storyboard template from our website, or create your own.

Installing
HUE Animation

If you already have your own stop motion animation software, you can skip these pages. If you don't, the software we use and recommend is HUE Animation.

Installing the software (Windows PCs)

Insert your software CD. If the installation screen doesn't appear automatically, browse to the CD in My Computer and double click on Menu.exe to launch the menu.

Follow the on-screen instructions to install the software. If you're prompted to confirm that you really want to install the software, click Yes. You may be asked to install some additional files if they aren't already on your computer. You will see a confirmation screen once installation is complete.

Now connect your HUE camera to an available USB port on the computer. You can launch the animation software from the Start Menu, the Charms Bar, or by clicking the shortcut on your Desktop.

Installing the software (Mac OS X)

Insert your software CD and double click on the installation file in the Mac folder.

Follow the on-screen instructions to install the software. On some versions of OS X, you may be prompted to enter your administrator's name and password. You will see a confirmation screen once installation is complete.

Now connect your HUE camera to an available USB port on the computer. You can launch the animation software from your Applications folder or through Spotlight.

> Note: If your computer doesn't have a CD drive, you can activate online at **register.hueanimation.com** to receive a software download link.

Activating Your Software

The final step is to activate your software. When you start it up you'll see a screen which looks like this.

To activate, you need to know your email address and your HUE code. If you received this book inside a HUE Animation Studio kit, you'll find your HUE code on the back cover (it will look a bit like this: HUE12345).

Check that you typed your email address correctly, then click OK. The software will take a few seconds to activate. Although you only have to activate once, it's best to keep your activation details in a safe place in case you get a new computer one day.

If it's the first time you're using the animation software, you'll also be asked to choose a Workspace folder. This is where your animation projects will be saved. The Default location will be best for most users. Click Select Folder (Windows) or Create Workspace (Mac) to continue.

The software will give you two options at the start: Create New Project or Open a Saved Project. Click the Create New Project icon, name your movie then click Save.

If you have any problems, please check the full Tutorials at **www.hueanimation.com**

PREFER TO ANIMATE ON THE MOVE? *Check out our iPad® app!*

Note: If you bought your software separately, you might have a license key instead of a HUE code. Follow the simple instructions in your license key email to activate the software.

Getting to Know the Software

This is what your camera is looking at.

If you're using HUE Animation, you should be looking at this screen after you've done all the start-up stuff. On the screen should be a picture of whatever your camera is pointing at.

This is your capture screen and it's where you'll be living as you make your movie. There are two buttons that you really need to know.

Playback
Click on this to play your movie.

Capture picture
Click on this to take your pictures.

No picture showing up?

Is your camera plugged in? Is it being used by another application (it will only work in one application at a time)? Double-check the USB connection to your computer at both ends. After you've checked your connections, go to the Camera menu at the top of your screen and select Refresh Camera.

Saving and sharing

To save your project so you can go back to work on it later, go to the File menu and select Save. If you have finished your animation and want to export it as a standalone movie file to share with your friends, go to the File menu and select Export. You can also upload your work straight to YouTube using the Share menu. See our online sharing tutorial if you need more help uploading your videos directly to the web.

Note: The software automatically saves your work regularly. As it is possible to make important changes in between automatic saves, we recommend that you save often to ensure that you don't ever lose any work.

What about all the other buttons on the screen?

You can add sound and do all sorts of editing tricks with the other buttons on the screen. We'll be talking about these buttons later in the book, but for now there are two ways to learn the basics about them:

• Use your first movie to test-drive the buttons

• Look at the video tutorials on the website: hueanimation.com/creations

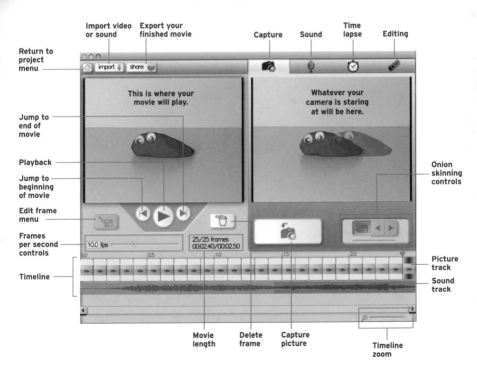

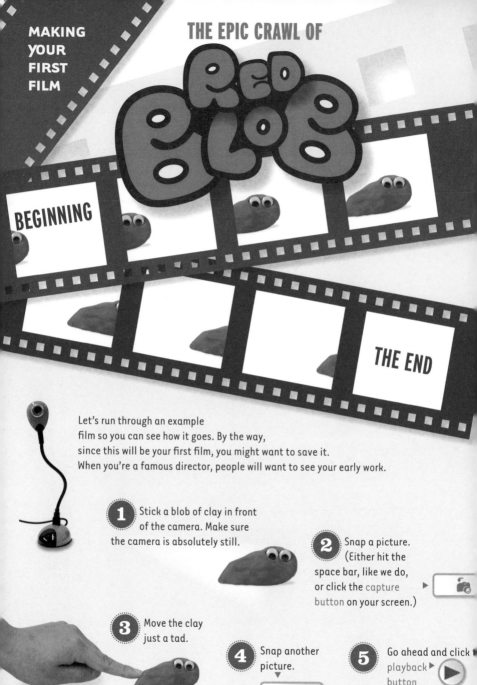

 MAKING YOUR FIRST FILM

THE EPIC CRAWL OF RED BLOB

BEGINNING

THE END

Let's run through an example
film so you can see how it goes. By the way,
since this will be your first film, you might want to save it.
When you're a famous director, people will want to see your early work.

1 Stick a blob of clay in front of the camera. Make sure the camera is absolutely still.

2 Snap a picture. (Either hit the space bar, like we do, or click the capture button on your screen.) ▶

3 Move the clay just a tad.

4 Snap another picture. ▼

5 Go ahead and click playback ▶ button right now. How's you movie look so far? (Answer? Short.)

 12

Here are the two screens you just used.

BEFORE taking the first picture

AFTER taking the first picture and getting ready to take the second

To take a picture, hit the space bar or click **here**. Your choice.

To lengthen your movie, move the clay another tad and snap another picture. You'll notice, by the way, that there are ghosts on the screen. Every time you move the clay, you'll see a "ghost" of where it used to be. This is called an "onion skin" of the old image and it's there to help you line up your new movement and keep the action smooth. Extremely helpful.

To finish your movie, repeat: Shoot, move, shoot, move, shoot, move... After a while, stop and push the playback button. Your first film! Congratulations!

THE END!

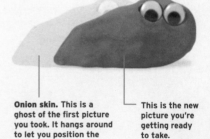

Onion skin. This is a ghost of the first picture you took. It hangs around to let you position the new picture.

This is the new picture you're getting ready to take.

Tips and Tricks

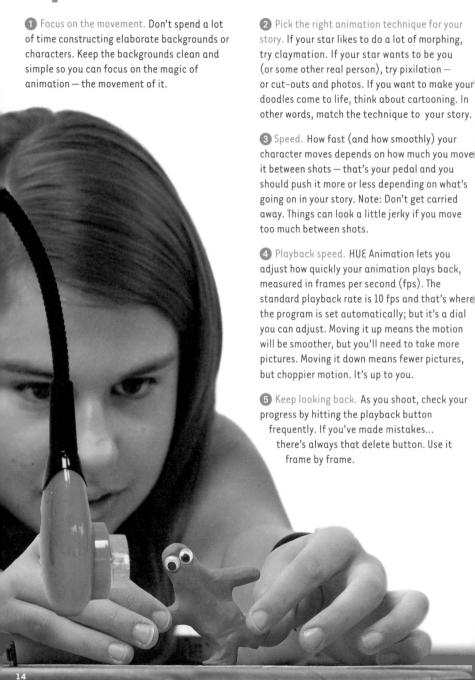

1 Focus on the movement. Don't spend a lot of time constructing elaborate backgrounds or characters. Keep the backgrounds clean and simple so you can focus on the magic of animation — the movement of it.

2 Pick the right animation technique for your story. If your star likes to do a lot of morphing, try claymation. If your star wants to be you (or some other real person), try pixilation — or cut-outs and photos. If you want to make your doodles come to life, think about cartooning. In other words, match the technique to your story.

3 Speed. How fast (and how smoothly) your character moves depends on how much you move it between shots — that's your pedal and you should push it more or less depending on what's going on in your story. Note: Don't get carried away. Things can look a little jerky if you move too much between shots.

4 Playback speed. HUE Animation lets you adjust how quickly your animation plays back, measured in frames per second (fps). The standard playback rate is 10 fps and that's where the program is set automatically; but it's a dial you can adjust. Moving it up means the motion will be smoother, but you'll need to take more pictures. Moving it down means fewer pictures, but choppier motion. It's up to you.

5 Keep looking back. As you shoot, check your progress by hitting the playback button frequently. If you've made mistakes... there's always that delete button. Use it frame by frame.

ANIMATION
STUDIO

QUICKSTART GUIDE

Guide de démarrage rapide • Schnellstartanleitung
Guida Rapida • クイックスタートガイド

Thank you
Merci
Vielen Dank
Grazie
ありがとうございました

Thank you for purchasing HUE Animation Studio. We hope you enjoy using this movie-making kit.

Please visit our website for additional information, FAQs, tutorials, and our full range of products.

We're always delighted to receive feedback about how you use your HUE products and reviews are most welcome.

We're here to help if you need us.

**With thanks
The HUE team**

When you see this symbol, you can find detailed instructions in The HUE Book of Animation.

Ce symbole indique que des explications pas à pas sont disponibles dans le Livre d'animation HUE (The HUE Book of Animation).

Wenn dieses Symbol erscheint, gibt es eine ausführliche Anleitung im HUE Buch der Animation.

Quando vedi questo simbolo, puoi trovare istruzioni dettagliate nel Libro HUE Animation (The HUE Book of Animation).

この印は、「The HUE Book of Animation」説明書のページ番号を示しています

installing hue animation

Installation de HUE Animation
Installation von HUE Animation
Installare HUE Animation
ソフトウェアインストール方法

Installing from CD

Avec CD d'installation
Installation mit CD
Installare da CD
CDからインストール

1. Insert the CD.
2. Open the installer menu.exe (Windows)
   or mac.dmg (Mac).

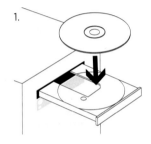

1.

2.

Menu.exe   Mac.dmg

Installing without a CD

Sans CD d'installation
Installation ohne CD
Installare senza un CD
CDを使わずにインストール

1. → huehd.com/registration
2. Create an account and register your code
   by clicking **Register New Software.**
3. Download the software installer and
   follow the onscreen instructions.

activating your software

Activation du logiciel
Aktivierung von HUE Animation
Attivare HUE Animation
ソフトウェアアクティベーション

Find your activation code.

Où trouver votre code d'activation ?
Wo finde ich meinen Aktivierungscode?
Trova il tuo codice d'attivazione.
アクティベーションコードは、本の裏表紙にあります。

The first time you activate, enter your email address and activation code.

Lors de la **première activation** du logiciel, entrez votre adresse e-mail ainsi que le code d'activation.

Wenn du die Software das **erste Mal** aktivierst, gib deine E-Mail-Adresse und deinen Aktivierungscode ein.

La prima volta che attivi, inserisci il tuo indirizzo email e il codice d'attivazione.

最初のアクティベーション時に、メールアドレスとアクティベーションコードを入力して下さい。

Alternatively, enter your email address and license key as shown.

Sinon, renseignez votre adresse e-mail et la clé de licence comme indiqué ci-contre.

Andernfalls gib deine E-Mail-Adresse und deinen Lizenzschlüssel ein wie hier abgebildet.

Altrimenti, inserisci il tuo indirizzo email e la chiave di licenza come mostrato.

または、メールアドレスとライセンスキーだけを入力して下さい。

You will be asked to select a Workspace for storing your files.

Vous devrez ensuite définir un espace de travail où sauvegarder vos fichiers.

Wähle nun einen Ordner aus in dem du deine Dateien speichern möchtest.

Ti verrà chiesto di selezionare un Workspace per archiviare i tuoi file.

プロジェクトを保存する「Workspace」フォルダを選択します。

about your camera

À propos de votre caméra
Über deine Kamera
A proposito della tua videocamera
カメラについて

Focusing ring
Mise au point
Fokussierung
Anello di messa
a fuoco
フォーカスリング

Microphone
Micro • Mikrofon
Microfono
内蔵マイク

Flexible neck
Tige flexible
Beweglicher
Kamerahals
Collo Flessibile
グースネック

Camera LED light
Voyant LED de la caméra
Kamera-LED
Luce LED della videocamera
カメラのLEDライト

USB cable
Câble USB
USB-Kabel
Cavo USB
ケーブル

Base LED light
Voyant LED du socle
Basis-LED
Luce LED della base
スタンドのLEDライト

Base
Socle • Basis
Base • スタンド

Focus your picture using the focusing ring
Ajustez manuellement la netteté de votre caméra grâce à la bague de mise au point.
Stell deine Kamera mithilfe des Fokussierrings ein.
Metti a fuoco la tua videocamera usando l'anello di messa a fuoco.
フォーカスリングを回してピントを合わせます

Create a stage with the box
Créez un décor en dépliant la boîte.
Baue aus der Schachtel deine erste Bühne.
Crea un palco con la scatola.
パッケージでミニステージを作成

starting your movie

Réaliser un film • Erstelle einen Film • Creare un film • 動画作成

1. Plan your story

You can print a storyboard
template from the CD.

Élaborez votre projet
Entwickle deine Geschichte
Pianifica la tua storia
ストーリーを組み立てる

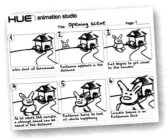

2. Set up your stage

Préparez la scène
Bereite die Bühne vor
Metti a punto il tuo palco
舞台を作る

3. Get to know your software

Familiarisez-vous avec le logiciel
Lerne die Software kennen
Prendi confidenza con il software
ソフトウェアに慣れておくと良いでしょう

4. Select your camera

Sélectionnez la caméra
Wähle die Kamera aus
Seleziona la videocamera
使用するカメラを選択する

5. Take a picture

Click the Capture Frame button (or the Space Bar),
then move the object and take another picture.
Prenez une photo
Mache ein Foto
Fai una foto
1コマずつ写真を撮る

 Capture Frame

adding sound
Son • Ajouter du son • Suono • オーディオ

Your CD contains sample sound effects

 Record Audio
Enregistrer une séquence audio • Audio aufnehmen
Registra Audio • 録音

 Click the Record Audio button to record sounds.
Click the button again to stop recording.

Cliquez sur le bouton rouge pour enregistrer du son. Cliquez à nouveau sur ce bouton pour arrêter l'enregistrement.

Drück auf den Record Audio-Knopf (Audioaufnahme), um Töne aufzunehmen. Drück ihn noch einmal, um die Aufnahme zu stoppen. Deine Audiodatei erscheint in der Zeitachse direkt unter deinen Bildern.

Clicca il bottone Record Audio (Registra Audio) per registrare suoni. Cliccalo ancora per fermare la registrazione. Il tuo file audio ti verrà visualizzato nella sequenza temporale sotto le tue immagini.

録音ボタンを押して録音を開始する。録音ボタンを再度押して録音を停止する。

You will see the audio file in the timeline below your images.

La piste audio s'affichera dans la barre temporelle sous vos images.

Deine Audiodatei erscheint in der Zeitachse direkt unter deinen Bildern.

Il tuo file audio ti verrà visualizzato nella sequenza temporale sotto le tue immagini.

オーディオを表した波形がタイムラインに表示されます。

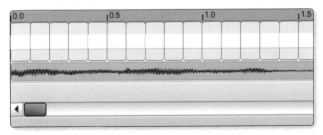

You can also import your own music or sound files.

 Import Audio
Importer un fichier audio • Audio importieren
Importa Audio • オーディオをインポート

adding text and graphics

Ajouter du texte et des illustrations • Texte und Bilder hinzufügen
Aggiungere testo e grafica • 編集ツール

Click this button to launch
the Edit frame functions ——→

Edit frame
Modifier les images
Bildbearbeitung
Modifica Fotogramma
コマ編集

Delete
Supprimer • Löschen
Cancella • 削除

Delete selected frames by
clicking this button

Manage Timeline
Gérer la barre temporelle
Zeitachse verwalten
Gestisci la Sequenza Temporale
タイムライン編集

 Reverse the order of
the selected frames
Inverser l'ordre des images.
Reihenfolge der Bilder
umkehren.
Inverti l'ordine dei
fotogrammi.
コマの順番を反転

 Adjust movie duration
to match audio
Ajuster la durée du film en
fonction du fichier audio.
Filmlänge an Audiolänge
anpassen.
Correggi la durata del film per
far corrispondere l'audio.
オーディオに合わせてフレーム
レートを自動的に設定

 Duplicate selected frames
Dupliquer les images
sélectionnées.
Ausgewählte Bilder duplizieren.
Duplica i fotogrammi selezionati.
コマを複製

 Duplicate audio track
Dupliquer les pistes audio
sélectionnées.
Ausgewählte Audiodateien
duplizieren.
Duplica la traccia audio selezionata.
オーディオを複製

fun things to try

Quelques idées amusantes • Lustige Ideen
Idee divertenti • コマ撮りテクニック

Time lapse

Prise de photo en time-lapse
Zeitraffer
Fotografia al rallentatore
タイムラプス（微速度撮影）

Set the frequency of frames taken and the duration of your movie.

Green screening (Chroma Key)

Incrustation sur fond vert (Chroma Key)
Greenscreen-Aufnahme
Fare un Green screen (Chroma Key)
クロマキー合成

See our tutorial "Using Special Effects and Chroma Key" **huehd.com/tutorials**

Disappearing act

Make something disappear by removing a small part closest to the ground each time you take a picture.

Faites disparaître des objets
Wie Dinge verschwinden und wieder auftauchen
Far apparire e sparire oggetti
魔法のように物を出現させたり消したりする

Filming from above

Place your background flat on the table and mount the camera above it.

You can also turn the camera upside down and flip/mirror the image in the Camera menu.

Tournage vu de dessus
Filmen von oben
Filmare da sopra
真上から撮影

saving and sharing

Enregistrer et partager vos réalisations
Speichern und Teilen • Salvare e condividere
保存・共有

You can save your project at any time by choosing Save from the File menu.

Enregistrez votre projet à tout moment en sélectionnant "Save" (Enregistrer) dans le menu "File" (Fichier).

Speichere dein Projekt indem du im "Datei"-Menü "Speichern" auswählst.

Salva il tuo progetto scegliendo Salva dal menu File.

「File」メニューから「Save」を選択して、プロジェクトを保存します

When your movie is finished, select Export from the File menu to create a movie file.

Lorsque votre film est terminé, sélectionnez "Export" (Exporter) dans le menu "File" (Fichier) pour créer un fichier vidéo.

Wähle im "Datei"-Menü "Exportieren" aus und erstelle eine Filmdatei.

Seleziona Esporta dal menu File per creare un film.

「File」メニューから「Export」を選択して、動画ファイルを作成します

To share your movie online, go to the Share menu or click the Share icon at the top of the screen. You can choose where you you'd like to upload your movie.

Pour partager votre film en ligne, allez dans le menu "Share" (Partager) ou cliquez sur l'icône "Share" en haut de la fenêtre. Choisissez ensuite où partager votre film.

Um deinen Film online zu teilen, ruf das "Teilen"-Menü auf oder klicke auf das "Teilen"-Symbol am oberen Bildschirmrand. Wähle nun aus, wo du deinen Film hochladen möchtest.

Per condividere il tuo film online, vai al menu Condividi o clicca l'icona Condividi in cima allo schermo. Puoi scegliere dove poter caricare il tuo film.

インターネット上で動画を共有するために、画面上にある「Share」メニューや「共有」アイコンを使用します。動画のアップロード先が選択できます。

sharing to Creatubbles™

Partager sur Creatubbles • Teilen auf Creatubbles
Condividere su Creatubbles • Creatubblesに動画をアップロード

Creatubbles is the safe global social network for teachers, children and parents focused on artwork and creativity. Save time, motivate children, and keep living portfolios of their work!

Creatubbles est le réseau social mondial sécurisé pour les enseignants, les enfants et les parents où la créativité et les arts visuels sont rois. Gagnez du temps, motivez les enfants et gardez des portfolios de leurs œuvres !

Creatubbles ist ein sicheres soziales Netzwerk für Lehrer, Kinder und Eltern bei dem Kunst und Kreativität im Mittelpunkt stehen. Sparen Sie Zeit, motivieren Sie die Kinder und behalten Sie lebendige Portfolios ihrer Arbeit!

Creatubbles è il sicuro social network per insegnanti, bambini e genitori incentrato su opere artistiche e creatività. Risparmia tempo, motiva i bambini e tieni vivi portfolio del loro lavoro!

「Creatubbles」（クリエイタブルズ）とは、クリエイティブな子どもたちのための安全なソーシャルプラットフォームです。
効率的に子どもたちのやる気をサポートしながら、作品ポートフォリオが作れます！

1. → **ctbl.es/HUEANIMATION**

2. Set up a Creatubbles account.

3. Follow the instructions on the previous page, choosing the Creatubbles option from the Share menu. You will need to log in.

4. Enter your movie's details then click Submit. You'll see a confirmation once your video is ready.

5. There may be a 'pending approval' banner on your creation while it's being reviewed, so take that time to check what other users have uploaded and leave feedback on their movies!

Pour des explications en français, rendez-vous sur :

Eine Anleitung auf Deutsch findest du unter dem untenstehenden Link:

Puoi trovare istruzioni in italiano al link sottostante:

詳細については以下のリンクをご参照ください：

huehd.com/creatubbles/tutorial

You can also upload single images and storyboards directly through the Creatubbles website.

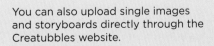

The HUE Book of Animation is also available in French and German. Check your online HUE account to download it.

Le Livre d'animation HUE est également disponible en français. Téléchargez-le depuis votre compte en ligne HUE.

Das HUE Buch der Animation ist auch auf Deutsch erhältlich. Sieh in deinem HUE Online-Konto nach und lade es herunter.

FR Pour plus d'informations, consultez le lien ci-dessous.

DE Weitere Informationen finden Sie unter dem untenstehenden Link.

IT Per maggiori informazioni consultare il nostro sito web al link sottostante.

JP 詳細については、以下のリンクをご参照ください

huehd.com/help

Want to use HUE Animation on your iPad or iPhone? Download our app!

Sound Effects

Animation without a sound track is like a song without the music - you get the idea but it's only half the show. When things fall down, fly away, slide on the ice, break the window, explode into atoms or just drop into a chair... you'll need the right bop, splat, ping, crunch, or bang to make it come alive.

Here are the two main ways to get sounds and music into your animation.

1 Record it yourself. You can bang your own pots and pans or record your own blood-curdling screams by using the microphone built into your camera.

Just click on the sound tab and then press the record button. Once you've recorded your sounds or music, it shows up on your timeline as an audio track and you can move it around to the right spot using your mouse.

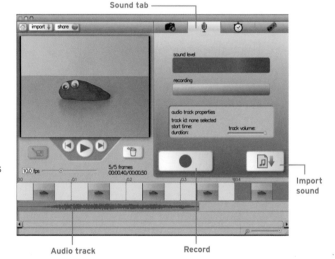

Sound tab

Import sound

Audio track

Record

2 Import the sound. HUE Animation allows you to import sound effects or music that you have on your computer. We recorded 12 classic sounds for you that will be useful making the projects in this book. We'll show you where to find them at hueanimation.com - or if you are using HUE Animation Studio, they will be included on your CD. You can also import audio files if you have your own collection. And then, of course, there's the web: Try a Google search for free libraries of music or sound effects. No matter where you get them, when you're ready to import a sound file, just click on the import sound button.

Model Car
Smashups

SCRIPT: Toy cars race around the room, smash into each other, fly off the tabletop, crash some more. The end.

INGREDIENTS: Two toy cars and some tape.

DIFFICULTY LEVEL
1

❶ Shoot.

❷ Move the cars a tad.

❸ Shoot again.

To animate a car race, follow the basic rule of animation: Move, shoot, move, shoot, move, shoot, move, shoot, move, shoot, move, shoot, move, shoot, and repeat.

Watch it
hueanimation.com/creations

How do I make the cars look like they're going faster?

Move them more between shots. The more you move them, the faster they look. Caution: If you move them too far, the motion gets jerky.

Slow

Scoot the car just a hair between shots.

Fast

Scoot the car a lot farther between shots.

How do I make the cars look like they're falling?

Use invisible tape to attach the cars to the wall. This makes them look like they're in mid-air, and it works a lot better than you might think. The tape disappears because of the movement.

The car reaches the end of the shelf and...

Tape the car to the wall. Shoot. Move.

!Kerpow!

Tape the car to the wall. Shoot. Move.

Choose your angles

Shoot from more than one angle to add excitement to the scene. Here are the three bas

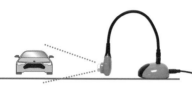

Shooting from profile

Shooting from the front

Shooting overhead

What's a tracking shot?

When the camera moves along with the target, that's called a tracking shot. Here the camera is moving along with the cars, but the angle is always profile.

How do I make sure the cars are lined up with the camera perfectly?

Before you shoot...

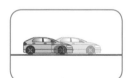

...scoot the camera and line the car up...

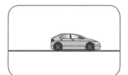

...with the "old" car that's been onion-skinned. Ready to shoot.

How to Do a Tracking Shot

Line the cars up with the camera, and shoot.

Move the camera and the cars. Use the onion skin to make sure the camera lines up with the cars again. Shoot.

Move the camera and the cars. Make sure the camera lines up with the cars again. Shoot.

Move the camera and the cars. Make sure the camera lines up with the cars again. Shoot.

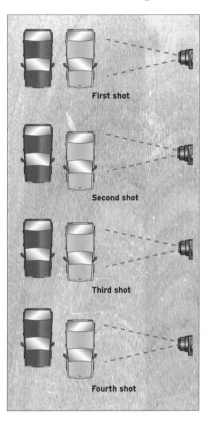

First shot

Second shot

Third shot

Fourth shot

THe NiGHTMARe BeFoRe BReAKFAST

SCRIPT: A short horror movie starring an evil spatula and a defenseless egg. A frying pan plays a supporting role.

INGREDIENTS: Egg, spatula, and frying pan.

DIFFICULTY LEVEL 1

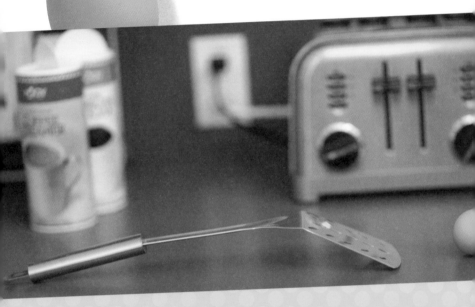

Chase scenes like this one are great places to practice the basic animation technique (shoot, move, and repeat). But they're also good places to understand that the basics can be played in a million different ways. Here, for example, we've used sound effects and a couple of angle changes to make a spooky drama. With different sound effects and angles, you could make a light-hearted romance. (Well, you might have to change the ending a little...)

When hints are inserted early in the story that suggest how the ending will go, filmmakers call it foreshadowing. For example, the shots in which the stove turns itself on and the frying pan slides into place are foreshadowings of tough times ahead for the egg. Very handy for building suspense. Keep it in your bag of tricks.

HOW TO SCARE AN EGG

To tell a good story in animation, you have to do more than just make things move around; you have to give them personalities. For example, don't just move the egg along in a steady motion. Have it hesitate, quiver, and then dart forward. You can also add sound effects such as soft whimpering or heavy breathing. Finally, try changing the angle to do a shot from the egg's point of view. This lets us feel what the egg feels when he takes a terrified glance back at the evil spatula.

Watch it
hueanimation.com/creations

Sizzle
Sizzle

SCRIPT: Our heroine compels a sandwich and a glass of juice to slide themselves down a long table. The two then mysteriously devour and drink themselves while she continues to fix them with baleful eyes.

INGREDIENTS: Actor. Snack.

No-Handed Eating

Since the real star of our show is the sandwich, we shot low and put the sandwich in the foreground. You can choose a different angle (over the shoulder, from the side, or overhead) for a different feel and to tell the story a different way. As the plate slides down the table (shoot, move, and repeat) we asked our heroine to stay completely still so she didn't move while the plate did. Incidentally, the sliding sound effects and the big chomping sound are hugely important. Use them proud and loud.

Watch it
hueanimation.com/creations

How to Get a Sandwich to Eat Itself

1 Shoot the sandwich.

CHOMP!

Sometimes you have to use a little imagination to record your sound effects. Try biting an apple instead of a sandwich to get a louder chomp. For the sliding sound, put a lot of weight on a plate and drag it across a counter. See page 15 for instructions on how to record and import homemade sound effects.

2 Take a bite.

Here's the ghost of the last shot you took. The onion skin. Use it as a guide to locate the sandwich for the next shot.

3 Put the bitten sandwich exactly back into place. You can be exact, by the way, because the onion skin provides you the guide.

4 Repeat.

RUNAWAY CLAY

SCRIPT: A red blob crawls out from a container and proceeds to baffle and terrorize its human victim before finally returning to its home, mischief accomplished.

INGREDIENTS: Actor, clay.

DIFFICULTY LEVEL
1

Clay is an animator's best friend, especially when the animator is — like we are — a little drawing-challenged. With clay, anybody can make a great-looking blobby monster and with the magic of animation, anybody can make it come alive.

1

Clay emerges from yellow container.

2

Cut to close-up.

3

Preparing to swat.

4

Clay oozes up between fingers.

Watch it
hueanimation.com/creations

24

Claymation® is probably the second-most common kind of animation (after cartooning). All the Wallace & Gromit™ films are done with clay characters, and countless internet films use the technique as well.

The preferred clay isn't the kind that comes out of the ground, by the way, it's, a formula originally developed more than one hundred years ago by an English art instructor.

Modelling clay doesn't dry out, doesn't flake, stain or melt in the sun. Most importantly, it shapes easily. Perfect for the job of animation.

Red blob attacks.

Red blob heads for cover.

Evades grasp.   Goes back home.

wink

To make your clay blob wink, flip over one of the googly eyes and draw a closed eye on the back. Add a ding sound effect.

CLAY HERO

SCRIPT: Our hero, The Blob Man, explores a desktop and has a series of office supply adventures.

INGREDIENTS: Actor. Random office supplies.

DIFFICULTY LEVEL 1

Check out the video online for our approach but don't worry about sticking to the script too closely. The reason we did it the way we did had mostly to do with the fact that we happened to have a stapler, paper clips, and a key on hand. If you only have a pair of scissors, a roll of tape, and a bent spoon, you should go with that and write a script accordingly.

To suspend him in the air, attach him to the wall using a pushpin.

Our hero bounces off stapler.

CLAY

Our hero emerges from his bowl.

He picks up a key and jams.

Cartoon Physics

Over the years animators have developed some tricks to make the physics of animation look better. Originally the goal was to get movements to look more realistic but animators quickly abandoned reality they found that exaggerated reality was funnier. That's why when you watch Saturday morning cartoons you'll notice that things boing, squash, and stretch more energetically than they do in the real world.

Watch it
hueanimation.com/creations

Here are a couple of the tricks of the trade:

Squash and Stretch

When your character is bouncing or jumping along he should squash and stretch as shown to give an exaggerated sense of weight and momentum.

Recoil

The recoil.   **The action!**

If your character is about to go from standing still to some energetic action like running, jumping, or throwing something, he should always first move away from his target before lunging forward. This helps prepare your audience for the motion to come and gives a sense of the force needed to lunge forward.

Ball in mid-air

Stretch in anticipation of impact

Squash on impact

Stretch as it takes off

Return to original shape in mid-air

He lands in cup of googlies and finally gets some eyes.

Paper clips make nice skates. Record yourself scraping paper clips along the table to get the ice skating sound.

CLAYVOLUTION

SCRIPT: Red Blob shows off its multiple personality disorder. Enters changing room and morphs in front of our eyes into a fish. Goes back inside and turns into a lizard, monkey, dog, and something else that's hard to tell exactly.

INGREDIENTS: Clay, googly eyes, and a cup.

DIFFICULTY LEVEL 1

CHANGING ROOM

1

2

Watch it
hueanimation.com/creations

How to make a fish morph into a blob before your eyes

Place your fish in front of the camera and take a frame. Pick him up and mold him a little bit. Use onion skinning to put him back exactly where he was. Take a frame. Repeat until your fish is a blob.

Some Random Ideas for Other Clay Adventures

• ClayMan scoots around on can-opener skateboard. Has unfortunate accident in which head gets badly flattened. Learns to cope by wearing skateboard for a hat. The end.

• ClayMan meets pencil-top eraser; falls in love. Eraser spurns him. He makes wish and morphs into matching eraser shape and tries again. Happy ending.

• ClayMan explores kitchen sink faucet. Disappears, re-emerges in new pipe-like shape. Sells movie rights. The end.

• Two clay blobketeers engage in paper clip sword fight. One loses head but eventually finds it and puts it back on. Backward. Comic ending.

3

5

4

6

A STICKY NOTE TALE OF FECAL REVENGE

Duck, Duck, Poop

SCRIPT: Duck flies over man and very deliberately poops on his head. Man goes airborne in outhouse and gets payback.

INGREDIENTS: A bunch of yellow sticky notes and a black marker.

DIFFICULTY LEVEL 2

SPLaT!

Watch it
hueanimation.com/creations

Get eight sticky notes and trace these ducks.

How to Make Your Bird Fly

1. On eight stickies, trace the eight ducks, conveniently numbered 1-8. See previous page.

2. Stick duck ① onto your background and shoot. Then pull it off.

3. Put duck ② where shown, and shoot. Repeat with ducks ③-⑧. Then go back to duck ① and do it all over again.

Trace the ducks.

Shoot the ducks in order, ①-⑧. Place them as shown.

How to Make Your Hero Wobble

Original   Tracing #1   Tracing #2   Tracing #3   Tracing #4

1. On a sticky note, draw a stick figure that looks sort of like ours. This becomes your original. Trace it three times.

2. Shoot the original and remove.

3. Put the first tracing in the same place. Shoot. Remove.

4. Repeat with the other tracings and cycle back to #1.

5. Since your tracings won't be exact, when you shoot them one after another the character will wobble a bit. A handy trick for adding personality.

The original

How to Make the Outhouse Door Open and Close

1. Draw an outhouse that looks sort of like ours, with the door closed.

2. On three more stickies, trace your outhouse, but on each sticky, open the door bit by bit. See the examples.

① ② ③ ④

3. Shoot the drawings in order ① ② ③ ④ to open the door. To close the door, shoot them ④ ③ ② ①.

How to Make the Balloon Inflate and the Outhouse Float Away

1. Draw a small balloon on a sticky note and stick this onto the top of the traced outhouse.

2. On another sticky note, draw a slightly larger balloon, and replace the smaller balloon.

3. Repeat two more times. Done.

4. To get the outhouse to float away, position them as shown and shoot them one at a time.

① ② ③ ④

THE END

33

Lawn Skating

SCRIPT: Our star skates across the lawn, performs a dramatic routine, then finishes with a lovely face-plant and slide-off.

INGREDIENTS: Actor. A big empty lawn.

DIFFICULTY LEVEL
2

When you make a real human being the star of your animation, you have a chance to make him or her do the impossible. In this case, that means skating across a lawn.

How to make the spin look real

Spin is faster with arms tucked in. Slower when arms are extended. Start upright and then spin into a crouch.

Watch it
hueanimation.com/creations

How to make the skating look real

1st shot

2nd shot

3rd shot

4th shot

↑ The back foot stays planted as you push off. The other foot moves forward.

Doesn't move. ↑   ↑ Moves.

Doesn't move. ↑   ↑ Moves.

↑ Now the back foot lifts, and you "coast" on the front foot.

Carpet Surfing

Invisible Car

IF you don't
want to
SKATE

The Stoolmobile

Bowling Ball Boy

Human Vacuum

36

Magic Carpet

Cross-Country
Handstanding

Garbage Can Races

on the LAWN

Here are more ideas. Shoot,
move, shoot, move, repeat...

Human Bobsled

MAGIC SHOES

SCRIPT: Man is enjoying a peaceful day in the park when he is approached by evil magic shoes. They drag him around, lift him off the ground, and then eventually drop him and steal the book.

INGREDIENTS: Actor. A big empty lawn. Shoes. Book.

Watch it
hueanimation.com/creations

1 First scene. The shoes approach and forcibly attach themselves to our hero's feet.

First shot   Second shot   Third shot, and so forth

2 Second scene. Make it look as if your hero is being dragged across the lawn by his shoes. Have him grab desperately at the grass. Shoot. Make him scoot backward. Shoot. Make him scoot backward. Shoot. Repeat.

First shot

3 Third scene. Our hero is still being dragged by his shoes, but this time they're pulling him into the air. This trick takes a little flexibility. Your hero has to kick his feet into the air, then you have to snap him at the highest point. It takes luck, practice, and timing. You can erase mistakes by selecting the frame where you got it wrong and hitting "delete."

Second shot

Third shot

Fourth shot

4 Fourth scene. Finally, our hero's shoes lift him off the ground and he flies. See next page for instructions!

HOW TO FLY

The hoverboard

One of the most impressive low-cost pixilation effects is the flying man routine. Check out our online video for the basic look. An ordinary-looking guy, with his legs tucked underneath him, levitates and floats across a lawn. (See Magic Shoes.) The trick takes timing, timing, timing. Your star has to jump and hit himself in the butt with his feet. And you, at the camera, have to catch the airborne moment, time after time. (The delete button is for the misses.)

Get ready to jump, and...

CLICK

Shoot.
Make your actor kick himself in the butt. It'll give him more air.

CLICK

Shoot.

Delete.
When you miss the moment, delete the frame and try again on the same spot.

CL
AN
DEL

More Flying Poses

When you're ready to move beyond the basics, try taping a piece of cardboard to your superhero's feet and getting him to hop. Catch him with the camera mid-air. A hoverboard!

Or get him to do the "jump-and-hit-own-butt routine," but with the added prop of a broom. Makes a great witch. Or use an umbrella and get the Mary Poppins look.

To do the helicopter, jump in place with your arms out, rotating slightly with each jump.

The witch

The helicopter

Harry Poppins

Watch it
hueanimation.com/creations

Shoot.

Shoot.
If you don't move far between jumps, you'll look like you're hovering. Very cool.

Shoot.

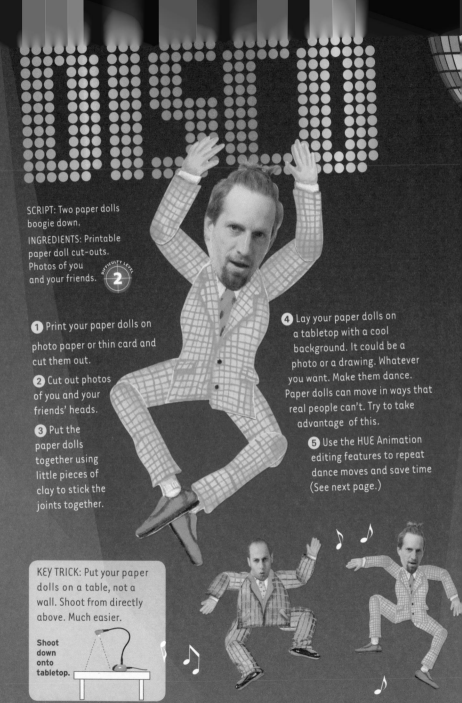

DISCO

SCRIPT: Two paper dolls boogie down.

INGREDIENTS: Printable paper doll cut-outs. Photos of you and your friends.

DIFFICULTY LEVEL
2

1 Print your paper dolls on photo paper or thin card and cut them out.

2 Cut out photos of you and your friends' heads.

3 Put the paper dolls together using little pieces of clay to stick the joints together.

4 Lay your paper dolls on a tabletop with a cool background. It could be a photo or a drawing. Whatever you want. Make them dance. Paper dolls can move in ways that real people can't. Try to take advantage of this.

5 Use the HUE Animation editing features to repeat dance moves and save time (See next page.)

KEY TRICK: Put your paper dolls on a table, not a wall. Shoot from directly above. Much easier.

Shoot down onto tabletop.

42

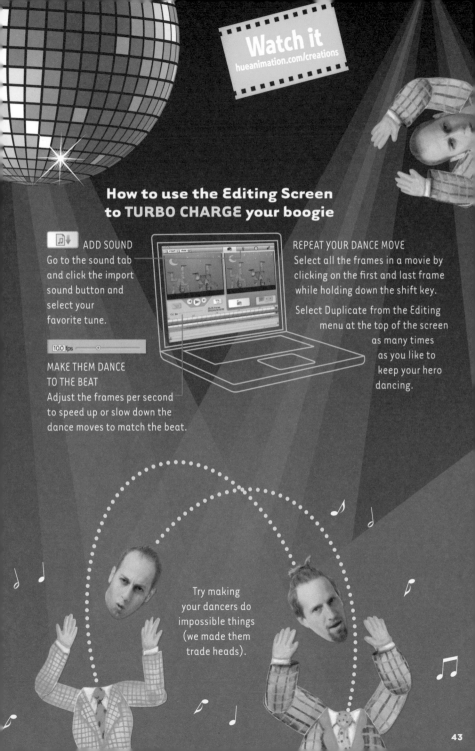

Watch it
hueanimation.com/creations

How to use the Editing Screen to TURBO CHARGE your boogie

ADD SOUND
Go to the sound tab and click the import sound button and select your favorite tune.

100 fps

MAKE THEM DANCE TO THE BEAT
Adjust the frames per second to speed up or slow down the dance moves to match the beat.

REPEAT YOUR DANCE MOVE
Select all the frames in a movie by clicking on the first and last frame while holding down the shift key.

Select Duplicate from the Editing menu at the top of the screen as many times as you like to keep your hero dancing.

Try making your dancers do impossible things (we made them trade heads).

famous FRUIT *Speeches*

SCRIPT: Classic speeches delivered by fresh fruit.

INGREDIENTS: Fruit, printable cut-outs, paper eyes (make your own).

DIFFICULTY LEVEL 2

Print out the two sets of mouths you're going to be using for this trick and cut them out. In each set, one mouth is wide open, one is closed, and one is midway. Your task will be to attach the lips to something that doesn't normally do much talking — we chose bananas and coconuts — and make them deliver some of the great speeches of all time. Check out the effect in the video.

YOU MAY THINK I'M JUST A BANANA BUT...

How to Get a Banana to Talk

1 You have a choice about where to get your audio track. You can record your own speech or song using the computer's microphone and the recording function in HUE Animation. Or you can import a real song or speech that you have on your computer. The import sound function is under the sound tab.

Record live sound

Import sound file

2 No matter where you got it, once you've imported your speech into HUE Animation, it will show up on your timeline. The next step is to match up the different mouth positions with the speech. To do this, first play back your audio track a few times and pay attention to how the talking lines up with the squiggly line in your audio clip. Then attach the different mouth positions to your banana and shoot them, matching loud talking with the open mouth, other kinds of talking with the middle mouth, and silence with the closed mouth.

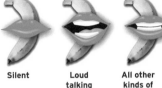

Silent   Loud   All other
              talking   kinds of
                            talking

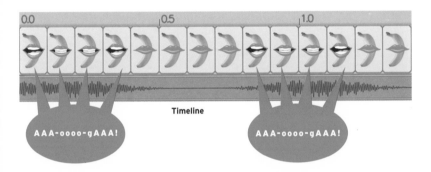

Timeline

AAA-oooo-gAAA!   AAA-oooo-gAAA!

Shortcut: Instead of shooting each mouth position multiple times, select Duplicate from the Editing menu at the top of the screen to duplicate the shots of each mouth position. Then drag them to the right place on the timeline.

3 The final step is to make minor adjustments by deleting a frame here and adding a frame there to get the speech and the mouth positions matched up precisely. The squiggly line on the audio clip is helpful for this step. Voila! Talking fruit.

I AM NOT
A CUKE!

Watch it
hueanimation.com/creations

First shot   Second shot   Third shot   Etc.

How to Make Nigel
TAKE A FALL

TAKE A WALK WITH NIGEL

DIFFICULTY LEVEL 1

1. Go to your CD or www.hueanimation.com and print all eight of these guys, then cut them out.

2. Place ① where shown, and shoot.

3. Remove ① and place ② where shown, and shoot.

4. Repeat with ③ through ⑧. At the ninth shot, cycle back to Nigel ①. You can make him walk forever by just repeating the cycle. Pretty nifty.

Waaahhhh!!

How to Make Nigel Fall from Book to Book

SCRIPT: Professor Nigel Plod walks in place on the cover of a book before leaving it and falling off the edge of a table into a series of other books which alter him in mysterious ways.

INGREDIENTS: Printable Nigel Plod cut-outs (wrapped in paper with your own titles on them), a table.

Watch it
hueanimation.com/creations

THE ADVENTURES OF NIGEL PLOD

HOW TO MAKE NIGEL WALK IN PLACE
Put Nigel ① on the cover of a book and shoot. Replace with Nigel ②. Shoot. Repeat with Nigels ③—⑧. To keep him walking, start all over again.

THE FRENCH REVOLUTION

HOW TO MAKE HIM LOSE HIS HEAD
Fold a piece of white paper and hook it over the top of the photo.

HOW TO MAKE HIM MULTIPLY
For this trick you need to put four Nigels into each shot. For the first shot, arrange as shown. For the second shot, replace number ④ with number ⑤, number ③ with number ④, number ② with number ③, and number ① with number ②. For the next shot, everyone continues to scoot down one spot. Repeat. A little parade of Nigels!

FUN WITH MULTIPLICATION

FLYING FOR THE HOPELESSLY EARTHBOUND

HOW TO MAKE THE BOOK FLY AWAY
Use fishing line.

①	②	③	④
For shot number 2 replace this one with ②.	Replace this one with ③.	Replace this one with ④.	Replace this one with ⑤.

? What other magical Nigel-transforming books can you think of?

space hero

SCRIPT: Our hero flies through space battling aliens. After an epic battle with an evil hole punch, he crash lands on a planet and miraculously recovers.

INGREDIENTS: Take a picture of yourself with a cape on and cut it out, or you can cut a superhero out of a comic book. You'll also need construction paper, googly eyes, the space background printout, and a stapler.

DIFFICULTY LEVEL
1

Boing

Place the cut-out on the space background printout (or some other background). Shoot, move, shoot, move, and repeat as always.

Make your hero punch out the space monsters and use the boing sound effect.

Make your own monsters by cutting them out of construction paper and attaching googly eyes with tape.

Watch it
hueanimation.com/creations

Whoosh!

Use the whoosh sound effect as your character zips across the galaxy.

Snap! Snap!

TIP 1

Shoot down onto a tabletop.

TIP 2

To make a mouth open and close, cut out two identical monsters, one with mouth shut, one with mouth open. Shoot and swap to make the mouth open and shut.

TIP 3

Try different backgrounds. Look for magazines with cool landscapes in them, or try having him fly across your refrigerator or a globe.

TIP 4

Take two shots like this, and swap them back and forth to make your character look at the camera.

Unmelting
ICE CREAM

SCRIPT: Plate full of sloppy white mess shapes itself into an ice cream sundae. Accompanied by orchestral score.

INGREDIENTS: Plate. Ice cream.

DIFFICULTY LEVEL
1

Time lapse photography allows you to see motion which would normally be too slow to notice. It's a kind of animation because it blurs a series of photographs into a moving image. But unlike other kinds of animation, all you have to do is set up the camera and walk away. Really easy. The trick is finding the right subject.

2:00

1:30

Here are a few other time lapse subjects you could try:

Busy street · Clouds · Your family at dinner · View out your window · Snails
Bread baking in the oven · Painting a picture · A fish tank

① TIME LAPSE

The time lapse screen

For this trick we used the time lapse tab in HUE Animation. ◄

We set it to take one frame every 30 seconds by putting the blue slider at 30s. Then we pushed the time lapse button. ►

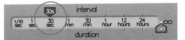

We moved the red slider to infinity. This means it will keep taking pictures until you tell it to stop.

② GOING BACKWARDS

First, select all the frames in the timeline by clicking Ctrl/A on a PC or Command/A on a Mac. Then select Reverse Frames from the Editing menu at the top of your screen to make the ice cream unmelt.

TA-DA!!

12:30

12:00

Watch it
hueanimation.com/creations

attack of the self-eating
SAND SNAKE

SCRIPT: A snake chases its prey in a circle and ends up swallowing itself.

INGREDIENTS: A handful of dry sand. Piece of black construction paper. An old toothbrush can help.

1 Spread your sand out on a piece of black construction paper. Spread the sand evenly using the side of a pencil.

2 Use an old toothbrush or something like it to clear a little circle of sand. Shoot.

3 Erase your little circle and make a new one a little farther along. Shoot again.

6 Have the snake lunge forward and close his jaws. He misses his prey the first couple of times.

7 The snake starts to eat himself!

8 The snake swallows himself whole and disappears.

DON'T HAVE ANY SAND?
You can animate with
anything you can scratch
off. Fill a cookie tray
with shaving cream and
scratch a drawing. Or use...
• Flour
• Finger paints
• Chocolate syrup

Watch it
hueanimation.com/creations

(4) Using a toothbrush,
clear out the sand to
make the outline of
a snake with his jaws
wide open.

(5) Make the snake chase
the little dot around
in a circle.

**IT'S ALL ABOUT
THE SOUND EFFECTS**
Pick a good chomping noise for your snake,
a good popping noise for when he swallows
himself up, and slide a penny around in the
sand to make the sound of the crawling snake.

Difficult trick but one of our favorites. You have to know your way around the computer pretty well to do this. Keep your plans modest and try a simple version of the trick first.

Magical, Moving Family Photos

SCRIPT: Family photos come to life, steal each other's hats, make faces, start a fight.

INGREDIENTS: Picture frames, a tall stack of photos that you'll have to shoot and print.

DIFFICULTY LEVEL
3

❶ Figure out what you want to happen in the picture frames and shoot it as video. Keep it simple and short. (Example: Girl waves, makes weird face, the end.)

import ↓ and share 🔵 buttons are up here.

❷ Import the video into HUE Animation by clicking the import button and selecting your video file. Then export it as a series of photos by going to the file menu at the top of your screen and selecting export and then image sequence.

20 seconds of video will give you 200 photos. That's about what we did, and that was plenty.

❸ Print out all of the photos on your printer. (It's easier if you put them all in one document and then print the document.)

You'll need a lot of paper and a lot of ink.

Remember, this trick is tricky. You really need to know your way around your computer.

Watch it
hueanimation.com/creations

OUR WALL IS REALLY A FLOOR
Set up a scene on your floor that looks like a wall. We put books and a plant on their sides and shot down on them from above.

Take the top photo from your stack, and place it in the frame. Then take a picture.

CLICK

Remove the photo and replace with the next one from your stack.

Then take a picture.

CLICK

CLICK

Do the same thing with the third picture...

...and the fourth...

...and so on. All the way through your stack. This will take a while, but it will be worth it. Check it out online.

CLICK

FOUR OTHER
PHOTO ANIMATION IDEAS

TALK TO YOURSELF
Take a series of photos of yourself in action. Print them out and shoot them one by one in a picture frame.

MAKE NIGEL WALK DOWN YOUR ARM
Tape Nigel to your arm and shoot the pictures in sequence as shown on page 47.

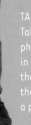

CEREAL BOX MOVIE
Use photo animation to make the picture on your cereal box come to life.

THE MAGIC BOOK
Make a moving picture book by taping a series of photographs into the book and shooting them one at a time.

Rotoscoping means turning video into animation.
We did it by tracing pictures right off
our computer screen.

ROTOSCOPING

SCRIPT: Balls juggle themselves, then a juggler magically
appears... balls and juggler change in mysterious ways.

DIFFICULTY LEVEL
3

INGREDIENTS: Pen and paper, markers.

1 Shoot some video.
Choose something that
loops, like juggling,
jumping rope, or
running in place.

2 Import the
video onto
your computer.

3 Play the video back full screen
and pause it.

4 Put a piece of typing paper over your
screen and outline the video with a
felt-tip pen. (It's important to use a
soft pen so you don't damage your
screen; no ball points!)

5 Advance the video forward about
three frames and trace it again on
a new piece of paper.

6 Repeat steps 4 and 5 until you have
completed a loop. (I.e., your juggler
is right back where he started with
ball number 1 in his right hand.)

TIP 1: Import the original sound from the video, and line it up with your drawings in HUE Animation software.

TIP 2: Don't worry about getting the drawings too precise. Messy drawings give your rotoscope a pleasant wobble.

7 Shoot your drawings in sequence in HUE Animation software. Adjust the frames per second to get the pacing to match the original video. If you drew every third frame it should be about right.

8 After you've shot all of your drawings select Duplicate from the Edit menu at the top of your screen to loop what you've done.

TIP 3: Try photocopying or tracing your drawings and coloring them in different ways to get variations on your original sketches.

Watch it
ueanimation.com/creations

Fun things to try

Turn the camera upside down

You can turn the camera upside down to get closer to the surface and then use the Flip Picture option in the Camera menu to rotate the image the right way around. With this trick you can get the camera very close to the ground.

Close ups

Make the rest of your animation and then film the close up shots right at the end. You can insert the frames into your timeline wherever you want them. This avoids having to move and re-focus your camera during filming. Take several photos of each close up so that the scene lasts longer in your movie (or use the Duplicate feature).

Film from above

Place the background flat on a table and mount the cable facing down onto the background image. Make sure that you have as much of the background in view as possible. This trick makes it easy to animate flight and other special effects.

Chroma Key (Green Screening)

Film your movie against a plain background. Once you finish taking pictures you can import photographs and use these as the background for your movie. So you could transport your characters to a desert or place them in front of a famous landmark like the Eiffel Tower in Paris.

Disappearing act

You can make something disappear into the ground by removing a small part of the object or character that is closest to the ground in between each shot. Make sure that you place the object back in the exact spot each time you remove a piece. The smaller the piece removed and the more shots you take, the better it will look.

Repeating and reversing frame sets

You might already know by now that you can highlight a group of frames and simply copy them to repeat the same action. You can take this a step further by using the Reverse Frames tool to reverse the sequence of frames you highlighted. This can make it look like someone is walking backwards or going around in a circle, back and forth. It's a great way of making your movie much longer with very little effort, and creating some fun effects at the same time.

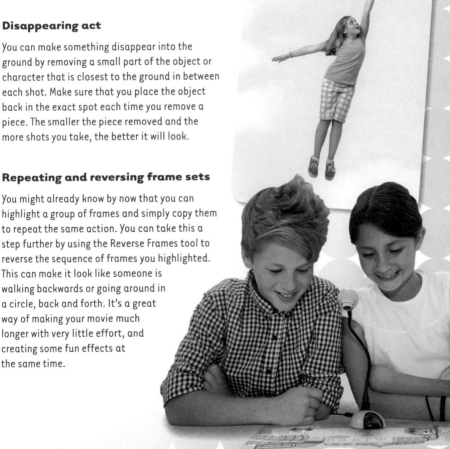

OTHER MOVIES WE'D LIKE TO SEE

Our hero gets a piece of tape stuck to foot, then hand, then head, then other hand... etc.

The molding tomato time-lapse: Take a picture of a tomato every day as it rots. Cover your nose!

Our hero shinnies down the phone cord to escape the evil scissorfish.

Our hero falls in love with a Barbie doll and is then turned into a frog by an evil troll doll.

Two animators made of clay make an animation about two animators made of clay making an animation about themselves.

You sit down to eat dinner but dinner slides across the table and molds itself into a big sloppy monster and eats you.

Our hero puts his foot into a binder-clip mouse trap and then tries to answer the phone and gets crushed.

You open the refrigerator door in the middle of the night and all the food is dancing. Then you start dancing and the food follows you out into the front yard and the whole neighborhood joins in.

Our hero is chasing a chicken across different landscapes and both hero and chicken turn from a doodle into clay into a photograph and into a rotoscope. A mix-up occurs and hero and chicken switch heads. They fight, reconcile, marry. The end.

About HUE Animation

Keep watching the HUE Animation website for more ideas, videos, competitions, help, tips and downloads. **www.hueanimation.com**

If your book came inside the HUE Animation Studio pack, did you know there are printable activities, storyboards, sound effects and backdrops on your installation CD?

PREFER TO ANIMATE ON THE MOVE? *Check out our iPad® app!*

Version 1.5.9
P/N: AB000X

Mac

Windows 8 Compatible

Contents:
HUE Animation software, animation movie examples and activity print-outs

ANIMATION STUDIO

Editors
John Cassidy & Nicholas Berger

Animator
Nicholas Berger (except for
The Nightmare Before Breakfast,
by Mike Attie)

Original Design (The Klutz Book
Of Animation) Kevin Plottner

Illustration
Liz Hutnick

Photography
Peter Fox

Nicholas Berger

Production
Patty Morris

Help
John Edmark

Brian Gravel, Chris Rogers and the
whole team at the Tufts University
Center for Engineering Education
and Outreach

The team at HUE

Craig Fry at Creativity, Inc.
David Malin

Inspiration
Preston Blair
Mike Jittlov

Caroline Leaf
Normal McLaren
George Méliès
Nick Park
Pes
Jan Svankmajer

Models
Tessa Barry, Laurel Fisher, Ava M.
Hallini, Marina Hallin, Anand Josh,
Sarah Limb, Alexandra Livingston,
Jordan Parker, Arturo Montes, Bill
Olson, Ashvin Srinivasan, Avery Zenger

Credits

Page 4: Chair © iStockPhoto.com/
FeodorKorolevsky
Page 4 and printouts: Ratoscope
(Phenakistoscope) © David Barker
Page 5, 20-21: Egg © iStockPhoto.com/
selensergen
Page 5: Snail © iStockPhoto.com/tomonikon
Page 7, 10: Laptop © iStockPhoto.com/CostinT
Page 20-21: Spatula © iStockPhoto.com/biosurf
Page 21: Frying pan © iStockPhoto.com/
bluestocking
Page 30: Duck © iStockPhoto.com/Chepko
Page 31-33: Pencil © iStockPhoto.com/NickS
Page 34-35: Grass © iStockPhoto.com/
webphotographeer
Page 42-43: Disco ball © iStockPhoto.com/
Kraska
Page 42-43: Spotlights © iStockPhoto.com/
deliormanli

Page 42-43 and printouts: Dancing Suits © Liz
Hutnick
Page 44-45 and printouts: Lips © Liz Hutnick
Page 44-45: Star banners © iStockPhoto.com/
angeal
Page 45: Cucumber © iStockPhoto.com/alex2
Page 46: Wood grain © iStockPhoto.com/
CreativeArchetype
Page 47: Wallpaper © iStockPhoto.com/billnc
Page 47: Small book © iStockPhoto.com/
fabphoto
Page 49: Hole puncher © iStockPhoto.com/
TokenPhoto
Page 49: Globe © iStockPhoto.com/kemalbas
Page 50: Ice cream scooper © iStockPhoto.
com/DNY59
Page 50: Clock © iStockPhoto.com/Viorika
Page 52: Hand © iStockPhoto.com/Nickilford
Page 53: Tray © iStockPhoto.com/Robinmaby
Page 53: Shaving cream © iStockPhoto.com/
antmagn
Page 54: Books © iStockPhoto.com/redmal
Page 55: Laptop © iStockPhoto.com/Colonel
Page 55: Printer © iStockPhoto.com/ambrits
Page 55-56: Paper stack © iStockPhoto.com/
Luso
Page 56: Paper sheet © iStockPhoto.
com/2happy
Page 57: Cereal box © iStockPhoto.com/
TheCrimsonMonkey
Page 62: Curtain © iStockPhoto.com/narvikk